WORDS *of* HOPE

WORDS *of* HOPE

Lisa Branning

WINEPRESS WP PUBLISHING

WinePress Publishing (PO Box 428, Enumclaw, WA 98022) functions only as book publisher. As such, the ultimate design, content, editorial accuracy, and views expressed or implied in this work are those of the author.

Unless otherwise noted, all Scriptures are taken from the *Holy Bible, New Living Translation,* copyright © 1996, 2004 by Tyndale Charitable Trust. Used by permission of Tyndale House Publishers, Wheaton, Illinois 60189. All rights reserved.

Scripture references marked NIV are taken from the *Holy Bible, New International Version®, NIV®.* Copyright © 1973, 1978, 1984 by the International Bible Society. Used by permission of Zondervan. All rights reserved.

Scripture references marked NKJ are taken from the *New King James Version,* © 1979, 1980, 1982 by Thomas Nelson, Inc., Publishers. Used by permission.

Scripture references marked NLV are taken from the *Holy Bible, New Life Version,* copyright 1969-2003 by Christian Literature International, P.O. Box 777, Canby, OR 97013. Used by permission.

ISBN 13: 978-1-57921-866-9
ISBN 10: 1-57921-866-0
Library of Congress Catalog Card Number: 2006904617

CONTENTS

Introduction • 1

Abandoned • 4
Scripture References • 5

Abused • 6
Scripture References • 7

Addictions • 8
Scripture References • 9

Afraid • 10
Scripture References • 11

Alcohol Addiction • 12
Scripture References • 13

Anger • 14
Scripture References • 15

Blessings • 16
Scripture References • 17

Brokenhearted • 18
Scripture References • 19

Church • 20
Scripture References • 21

Comfort • 22
Scripture References • 23

Death • 24
Scripture References • 25

Delight • 26
Scripture References • 27

Depression • 28
Scripture References • 29

Discouraged • 30
Scripture References • 31

Divorce • 32
Scripture References • 33

Eternal Life • 34
Scripture References • 35

Faith • 36
Scripture References • 37

Forgiveness • 38
Scripture References • 39

God Cares • 40
Scripture References • 41

Godliness • 42
Scripture References • 43

God's Will • 44
Scripture References • 45

God's Love • 46
Scripture References • 47

God's Word • 48
Scripture References • 49

Guidance • 50
Scripture References • 51

Hearts • 52
Scripture References • 53

Holy • 54
Scripture References • 55

Holy Spirit • 56
Scripture References • 57

Hope • 58
Scripture References • 59

Husbands • 60
Scripture References • 61

Integrity • 62
Scripture References • 63

Joy • 64
Scripture References • 65

Lukewarm Spiritually • 66
Scripture References • 67

Marriage • 68
Scripture References • 69

Nation • 70
Scripture References • 71

Obedience • 72
Scripture References • 73

Orphans and Widows • 74
Scripture References • 75

Peace • 76
Scripture References • 77

Pleasing God • 78
Scripture References • 79

Praise and Worship • 80
Scripture References • 81

Prayer • 82
Scripture References • 83

Praying for My Children • 84
Scripture References • 85

Praying for My Husband • 86
Scripture References • 87

Praying for My Wife • 88
Scripture References • 89

Protection • 90
Scripture References • 91

Salvation • 92
Scripture References • 93

Salvation for Everyone • 94
Scripture References • 95

Salvation for Family and Friends • 96
Scripture References • 97

Satan Defeated • 98
Scripture References • 99

Seeking God • 100
Scripture References • 101

Sexual Immorality • 102
Scripture References • 103

Sickness • 104
Scripture References • 105

Sorrow • 106
Scripture References • 107

Spiritual Growth • 108
Scripture References • 109

Strength • 110
Scripture References • 111

Suffering • 112
Scripture References • 113

Temptation • 114
Scripture References • 115

Tithing • 116
Scripture References • 117

Troubles • 118
Scripture References • 119

Trust • 120
Scripture References • 121

Wisdom • 122
Scripture References • 123

Wives • 124
Scripture References • 125

Worried • 126
Scripture References • 127

Youth • 128
Scripture References • 129

Author's Testimony • 131

INTRODUCTION

The purpose of this prayer devotional is to help people to know God intimately. To be intimate with God you need to spend time seeking him in prayer and in his word. My hope is that as you pray these scripture prayer devotionals you will meditate on the words, which are God's words to you. As God's words penetrate your heart and mind, you will begin to think the thoughts God desires you to think. Often our thoughts about a situation are negative. We need to replace our thoughts with God's thoughts, which are full of hope, and they give us the comfort and the strength we need. God loves you immensely and he has given you his word to learn about him and to encourage you as you live in this world. When you are going through any situation and you pray scripture, God will give you the wisdom you need to make the right choices and decisions that are his will for you. God's word is filled with many wonderful promises he has made to you and me. The most important promise is that he loves us. Paul prays for the Ephesians, and I pray this for you. "I pray that you being rooted and established in love, may have power, together with all the saints, to grasp how wide and long and high and deep is the love of Christ, and to know this love that surpasses knowledge, that you may be filled to the measure of all the fullness of

God" (Eph. 3:17–19). God's word says in Mark 12:30, "Love the Lord your God with all your heart and with all your soul and with all your mind and with all your strength." God desires you to love him and for you to seek to know him. As you spend time with him, he will pour his love into your heart and give you his peace. Life is hard, but you can trust God to take care of you when you give your life to him. God will never leave you or forsake you. He will always love you.

I pray this book will give hope to everyone who reads it, especially if you have been hurt or brokenhearted. God is your loving Father and he is the only one you can depend on all the time. He is always with you. God wants you to pray to him and talk to him about everything going on in your life. He will answer your prayers in wonderful ways, beyond what you ask, or think. God knows what is best for you. Commit everything to him, trust him, and he will help you. God is your refuge and place of safety. He will never abandon you. May God richly bless your life with his unfailing love.

ABANDONED

God, I pray you will turn to me and have mercy on me, for I am alone and in deep distress. Feel my pain and see my trouble. Look down upon my sorrows and rescue me. I know you are merciful and you will not abandon me. For those who know your name trust in you, for you, O Lord, have never abandoned anyone who searches for you. You will never fail me or forsake me. I know it is better to trust you than to put my confidence in people. For my life is precious to you. You are my loving ally and my fortress, my tower of safety, my deliverer. I praise you Lord, for you have shown me your unfailing love. You are my light; you light up my darkness. Even if my father and mother abandon me, you will hold me close. You will never abandon me. I know you are always with me, granting me the joy of your presence forever. Each day you carry me in your arms. You shelter me in your presence. I pray I will trust in you and that I will put my hope and confidence in you. For your love for me is very great.

SCRIPTURE REFERENCES

Psalm 25:16
Psalm 25:18
Psalm 119:153
Deuteronomy 4:31
Psalm 9:10
Hebrews 13:5
Psalm 118:8
Psalm 72:14
Psalm 144:2
Psalm 31:21
2 Samuel 22:29
Psalm 27:10
2 Corinthians 4:9
Psalm 16:8
Psalm 16:11
Psalm 68:19
Psalm 31:20
Jeremiah 17:7
Psalm 86:13

ABUSED

God, I pray you will rescue me, and that I will no longer be abused. My heart is in anguish. I cry to you for help, for my heart is overwhelmed. Lead me to the towering rock of safety, for you are my safe refuge. God, you hear my cries; you look down and feel deep concern for my welfare. You will help the oppressed, who have no one to defend them. You will bind up my injuries and strengthen me. For you stand beside the needy, ready to save me. You surround me with your love and your tender mercies. I thank you Lord with all my heart. Help me, O Lord my God! Save me because of your unfailing love. Rescue me, because you are so faithful and good. I will trust in your unfailing love. I will rejoice because you have rescued me. For you know the plans you have for me. They are plans for good and not for disaster, to give me a future and a hope. I pray I will wait quietly before you, for my hope is in you. You alone are my rock and my salvation. My fortress where I will not be shaken.

SCRIPTURE REFERENCES

Ezekiel 34:22

Psalm 55:4

Psalm 61:2, 3

Exodus 2:24, 25

Psalm 72:12

Ezekiel 34:16

Psalm 109:31

Psalm 103:4

Psalm 111:1

Psalm 109:26

Psalm 109:21

Psalm 13:5

Jeremiah 29:11

Psalm 62:5, 6

ADDICTIONS

*(Drugs, sexual, smoking, eating,
gambling, shopping, etc.)*

God, I pray that you will give me a new heart with new and right desires. Take out my stony heart of sin and give me a new, obedient heart. I need to keep alert and pray. Otherwise temptation will overpower me. For though the spirit is willing enough, the body is weak. When I pray, you answer me; you encourage me by giving me the strength I need. Though I stumble, I will not fall, for you hold me by my hand. I give you my burdens (including my addictions) for I know you will take care of me. I need to be strong and take courage, for I can do everything with the help of Christ your Son who gives me the strength I need. For you show me the proper path when I go astray. I will throw off my old evil nature because I am a new person, created in your likeness—righteous, holy, and true. I pray I will not yield to temptation, and that you will deliver me from the evil one. I will seek to do your will in all I do, and you will direct my paths. I will store your commands in my heart, for they will give me a long and satisfying life. And I am sure that you will continue your work until it is finished on that day when Christ Jesus comes back again. I praise you and give you thanks, for you are good! Your faithful love endures forever.

SCRIPTURE REFERENCES

Ezekiel 36:26

Mark 14:38

Psalm 138:3

Psalm 37:24

Psalm 55:22

Psalm 31:24

Philippians 4:13

Psalm 25:8

Ephesians 4:22

Ephesians 4:24

Matthew 6:13

Proverbs 3:6

Proverbs 3:1, 2

Philippians 1:6

Psalm 106:1

AFRAID

God, I pray I will be strong and courageous! That I will not be afraid or discouraged. For you, Lord, are with me wherever I go. You are my light and salvation, so why should I be afraid? You protect me from danger. But when I am afraid, I will put my trust in you. I will be strong and not fear. For you are coming to save me. And you will open wide the gates of heaven for me to enter into the eternal kingdom of my Lord and Savior Jesus Christ. So I won't be afraid, for it gives you, my Father, great pleasure to give me the kingdom. You will give me all I need from day to day if I make your kingdom my primary concern. You will never fail me or forsake me. That is why I can say with confidence: you are my helper, so I will not be afraid. You are my strength and my song, and you have become my victory. You tell me, "Don't be afraid, for I am with you. Do not be dismayed, for I am your God. I will strengthen you. I will help you. I will uphold you with my victorious right hand." I pray I won't be afraid, for I am deeply loved by you. I will be at peace, take heart, and be strong!

SCRIPTURE REFERENCES

Joshua 1:9

Psalm 27:1

Psalm 56:3

Isaiah 35:4

2 Peter 1:11

Luke 12:32

Luke 12:31

Hebrews 13:5, 6

Psalm 118:14

Isaiah 41:10

Daniel 10:19

ALCOHOL ADDICTION

God, I pray I will be decent and true in everything I do. That I would not participate in wild parties and getting drunk. But that I would let the Lord Jesus Christ take control of me, and not think of ways to indulge my evil desires. I need to not get drunk on wine, because it will ruin my life. Instead, let the Holy Spirit fill and control me. God, you are faithful. You will keep the temptation from becoming so strong that I can't stand up against it. When I am tempted, you will show me a way out, so that I will not give in to it. So I will be strong and take courage. For I can do everything with the help of Christ who gives me the strength I need. God, I confess my sins to you. You are faithful and just to forgive me and to cleanse me from every wrong. I pray I will not let any part of my body become a tool of wickedness, to be used for sinning. Instead, that I would give myself completely to you, God, since you have given me new life. I need to use my whole body as a tool to do what is right for your glory. God, transform me into a new person by changing the way I think. Then I will know what you want me to do, and I will know how good and pleasing and perfect your will really is. I look to you for help and I will trust in your unfailing love. I will rejoice because you have rescued me and you are my refuge and strength.

SCRIPTURE
REFERENCES

Romans 13:13, 14
Ephesians 5:18
1 Corinthians 10:13
Psalm 31:24
Philippians 4:13
1 John 1:9
Romans 6:13
Romans 12:2
Psalm 141:8
Psalm 13:5
Psalm 46:1

ANGER

God, I pray I will not sin by letting anger gain control over me. I need to not let the sun go down while I am still angry. For anger gives a mighty foothold to the devil. I need to get rid of all bitterness, rage, anger, harsh words, and slander, as well as all types of malicious behavior and abusive language. When I control my anger I will have understanding, but when I have a hasty temper I will make mistakes. My tongue can kill or nourish life. Gentle words bring life and health; a deceitful tongue crushes the spirit. A gentle answer turns away wrath, but harsh words stir up anger. I pray I will have good sense and restrain my anger. And that I would be kind, tenderhearted, and forgiving, just as you are, God. That I would be humble, gentle, and patient, making allowances for other's faults because of your love. May love be my highest goal. Love is patient and kind. Love is not jealous, or boastful, or proud, or rude. Love does not demand its own way. Love is not irritable, and it keeps no record of when it has been wronged. Love never gives up, never loses faith, is always hopeful, and endures every circumstance. I pray for those who have hurt me: that I will love them, and that as I live in you, God, my love will grow more perfect.

SCRIPTURE REFERENCES

Ephesians 4:26, 27

Ephesians 4:31

Ephesians 4:29

Proverbs 14:29

Proverbs 18:21

Proverbs 15:4

Proverbs 15:1

Proverbs 19:11

Ephesians 4:32

Ephesians 4:2

1 Corinthians 14:1

1 Corinthians 13:4, 5

1 Corinthians 13:7

Luke 6:28

John 13:34

1 John 4:17

BLESSINGS

God, I pray I will trust in you and make you my hope and confidence. You bless those who realize their need for you, for the kingdom of heaven will be given to them. I need to think clearly, exercise self-control and look forward to the special blessings that will come to me at the return of Jesus Christ my Savior. For he will come as unexpectedly as a thief! I will be blessed if I am watching for him. So I won't get tired of doing what is good. I won't get discouraged and give up, for I will reap a harvest of blessing at the appropriate time. For you search all hearts and examine secret motives. You give all people their due rewards, according to what their actions deserve. God, you bless those whose hearts are pure, and they shall see you. The godly are showered with blessings, and you surround them with your shield of love. How I praise you, God, the Father of my Lord Jesus Christ, who has blessed me with every spiritual blessing in the heavenly realms, because I belong to Christ. With all my heart I want your blessings. My heart rejoices in you. I pray I will bless you everyday and praise you forever.

SCRIPTURE REFERENCES

Jeremiah 17:7

Matthew 5:3

1 Peter 1:13

Revelation 16:15

Galatians 6:9

Jeremiah 17:10

Matthew 5:8

Proverbs 10:6

Psalm 5:12

Ephesians 1:3

Psalm 119:58

1 Samuel 2:1

Psalm 145:2

BROKENHEARTED

God, I pray you will see my anguish! My heart is broken and my heart despairs. Please listen to my cry! Hear my prayer! You are close to the brokenhearted; you rescue those who are crushed in spirit. I pour out my heart to you, for you are my refuge. I have cried until the tears no longer come. In your faithful love, O Lord, hear my cry. Look down upon my sorrows and rescue me. Have compassion on me, for I am weak! Heal me, for my body is in agony. I am sick at heart. O Lord, you alone can heal me, you alone can save me. You heal the brokenhearted, binding up their wounds. When I pray, you answer me; you encourage me by giving me the strength I need. How kind you are! So merciful, you are the source of every mercy, and you comfort me. You love me with unfailing love. Your unfailing love surrounds those who trust in you. I pray I will trust in you with all my heart.

SCRIPTURE REFERENCES

Lamentations 1:20
Psalm 61:1
Psalm 34:18
Psalm 62:8
Lamentations 2:11
Psalm 119:149
Psalm 119:153
Psalm 6:2, 3
Jeremiah 17:14
Psalm 147:3
Psalm 138:3
Psalm 116:5
2 Corinthians 1:3
Psalm 117:2
Psalm 32:10
Proverbs 3:5

CHURCH

God, I pray for my church; that the pastors, church leaders, and teachers will feed and shepherd your flock—the church, purchased with Christ's blood. That no one will distort the truth. May we hold to the truth in love, becoming more and more in every way like Christ, who is the head of his body, the church. Under his direction, the whole body is fitted together perfectly. As each part does its own special work, it helps the other parts grow, so that the whole body is healthy and growing and full of love. I pray we will get rid of all bitterness, rage, anger, harsh words, and slander, as well as all types of malicious behavior. That we would be kind to each other, tenderhearted, forgiving one another just as you, God, through Christ have forgiven us. Let us aim for harmony in our church and try to build each other up. We need to give our bodies to you and let them be a living and holy sacrifice—the kind you will accept. I pray we will not copy the behavior and customs of this world, but let you transform us into a new person by changing the way we think. Then we will know what you want us to do, and we will know how good your will really is. May you, God, be given glory in our church and in Christ Jesus forever.

SCRIPTURE REFERENCES

Acts 20:28
Acts 20:30
Ephesians 4:15, 16
Ephesians 4:31, 32
Romans 14:19
Romans 12:1, 2
Ephesians 3:21

COMFORT

God, I pray your unfailing love will comfort me. You are close to the brokenhearted; you rescue those who are crushed in spirit. Lord you hear me when I call to you for help. You are my safe place and my strength; you always help me when I am in trouble. When doubts fill my mind, your comfort gives me renewed hope and cheer. You are my place of refuge. You are all I really want in life. I thank you with all my heart. May my Lord Jesus Christ and you, God my Father, who have loved me and in your special favor gave me everlasting comfort and good hope, comfort my heart and give me strength in every good thing I do and say. Lord you are my shepherd, I have everything I need. You let me rest in green meadows; you lead me beside peaceful streams. You renew my strength and restore my soul. You guide me along right paths, bringing honor to your name. To you, O Lord, I lift up my soul. You are the source of every mercy. I pray I will trust you at all times and that I will pour out my heart to you. For you are my God who comforts me. I love you with all my heart.

SCRIPTURE
REFERENCES

Psalm 119:76

Psalm 34:18

Psalm 34:17

Psalm 46:1 NLV

Psalm 94:19

Psalm 142:5

2 Thessalonians 2:16, 17

Psalm 23:1–3 NLT, NIV

Psalm 25:1

2 Corinthians 1:3

Psalm 62:8

Psalm 103:4

Psalm 106:1

Psalm 111:1

DEATH

God, I pray you will show me the way of life, granting me the joy of your presence and the pleasures of living with you forever. Even when I walk through the dark valley of death, I will not be afraid, for you are close beside me. You alone are my refuge, my place of safety; you are my God, and I am trusting you. You are my eternal Rock. You nurse me when I am sick and ease my pain and discomfort. I love you because you hear and answer my prayers. Because you bend down and listen, I will pray as long as I have breath! Jesus said, "I am the resurrection and the life. Those who believe in me, even though they die like everyone else, will live again. They are given eternal life for believing in me and will never perish. There are many rooms in my Father's home, and I am going to prepare a place for you." God, you will live with us, and we will be your people. You will remove all of our sorrows, and there will be no more death, or sorrow, or crying, or pain. For the old world and its evils will be gone forever. To all who are thirsty, you will give the spring of the water of life without charge. All who are victorious will inherit all these blessings and you will be their God, and we will be your children. I thank you for answering my prayer and saving me! I praise you from the bottom of my heart.

SCRIPTURE REFERENCES

Psalm 16:11

Psalm 23:4

Psalm 91:2

Isaiah 26:4

Psalm 41:3

Psalm 116:1, 2

John 11:25, 26

John 14:2

Revelation 21:3, 4

Revelation 21:6

Psalm 118:21

Psalm 35:10

DELIGHT

God, I pray I will delight in doing everything you want and that day and night I will think about your law. Yes, happy are those who delight in doing what you command. Lord, you will rejoice over me for good if I obey your voice and keep your commandments and statutes, and if I turn to you with all my heart and with all my soul. You ask me to give you my heart and that my eyes would delight in your ways of wisdom. I pray I will hide your word in my heart that I might sin against you. For light shines on the godly and joy on those who do right. The steps of the godly are directed by you, and you delight in every detail of their lives. When I delight in you, Lord, you will give me my heart's desires. Your delight is in those who honor you and put their hope in your unfailing love. I will delight myself in you, my Almighty God.

SCRIPTURE REFERENCES

Psalm 1:2

Psalm 112:1

Deuteronomy 30:9, 10 NKJ

Proverbs 23:26

Psalm 119:11

Psalm 97:11

Psalm 37:23

Psalm 37:4

Psalm 147:11

Job 22:26

DEPRESSION

God, I pray you will answer my prayers, for your unfailing love is wonderful. Please turn and take care of me. For you, Lord, hear the cries of your needy ones. And now my heart is broken. Depression haunts my days. Come quickly, Lord, and answer me, for my depression deepens. Lord, don't hold back your tender mercies from me. My only hope is in your unfailing love and faithfulness. Your unfailing love is better to me than life itself; how I praise you! For you bless the godly, O Lord, surrounding them with your shield of love. I pray I will not be afraid for I am deeply loved by you. I will be at peace and take heart and be strong. For your eyes watch over those who do right. Your ears are open to my cries for help. You rescue me from all my troubles. Jesus, you tell me to come to you when I am weary and carry heavy burdens, and you will give me rest for my soul. God sent you to comfort the broken-hearted. I know you are always with me. I will not be shaken, for you are right beside me. For each day you carry me in your arms. Your goodness is so great!

SCRIPTURE
REFERENCES

Psalm 69:16

Psalm 69:33

Job 30:16

Psalm 143:7

Psalm 40:11

Psalm 63:3

Psalm 5:12

Daniel 10:19

Psalm 34:15

Psalm 34:17

Matthew 11:28, 29

Isaiah 61:1

Psalm 16:8

Psalm 68:19

Psalm 31:19

DISCOURAGED

God, I pray I will not be afraid or discouraged. For you, the Lord my God, are with me wherever I go. Why am I discouraged? Why so sad? I will put my hope in you! I will praise you again, my Savior and my God! When I pray, you answer me. You encourage me by giving me the strength I need. Those who wait on you will find new strength. They will fly high on wings like eagles and not faint. Those who live in the shelter of the Most High will find rest in the shadow of the Almighty. O my Strength, to you I sing praises, for you are my refuge, my God who shows me unfailing love. You give power to those who are tired and worn out; you offer strength to the weak. I will boast only in you, Lord. Let all who are discouraged take heart. You are my strength, my shield from every danger. I trust you with all my heart. You help me and my heart is filled with joy. For I can do everything with the help of Christ who gives me the strength I need. I pray I will be strong and take courage. I will put my hope in you.

SCRIPTURE
REFERENCES

Joshua 1:9

Psalm 42:5

Psalm 138:3

Isaiah 40:31

Psalm 91:1

Psalm 59:17

Isaiah 40:29

Psalm 34:2

Psalm 28:7

Philippians 4:13

Psalm 31:24

DIVORCE

God, I pray we will give honor to our marriage, and remain faithful to one another. We need to keep ourselves pure and seek to live a clean and holy life. May we submit to one another out of reverence for Christ. We need to be wise with spiritual wisdom, and then we will live wisely and be pure. God you want us to be holy, so we should keep clear of all sexual sin. For you will surely judge people who are immoral and those who commit adultery. You say, "I hate divorce! It is as cruel as putting on a victim's bloodstained coat." A man who divorces his wife and marries another woman commits adultery, unless his wife has been unfaithful. And if a woman divorces her husband and remarries, she commits adultery. I pray we will allow the Holy Spirit to control our lives; when we do he will produce in us love, joy, peace, patience, kindness, goodness, faithfulness, gentleness, and self control. We need to really love each other intensely with all our hearts. Help us to be humble and gentle with each other and to be patient, making allowances for each other's faults because of your love for us. I thank you for surrounding us with your love and tender mercies.

SCRIPTURE REFERENCES

Hebrews 13:4
2 Timothy 3:21
Hebrews 12:14
Ephesians 5:21
Colossians 1:9
Titus 2:5
Galatians 5:22, 23
1 Peter 1:22
Ephesians 4:2
Psalm 111:1
Psalm 103:4

ETERNAL LIFE

God, I pray I will live in such a way that your love can bless me, as I wait for the eternal life that my Lord Jesus Christ in his mercy is going to give me. For you, God, so loved the world that you gave your only Son, so that everyone who believes in him will not perish but have eternal life. For if I confess with my mouth that Jesus is Lord and believe in my heart that you raised him from the dead, I will be saved. God, you will give eternal life to those who persist in doing what is good, seeking after the glory and honor and immortality that you offer. I will trust in you always, for you are my eternal Rock. I can rejoice in my wonderful new relationship with you, all because of what my Lord Jesus Christ has done for me in making me friends with you, my God. Thank you for your Son, a gift too wonderful for words! I will humble myself and pray and seek your face and turn from my wicked ways. Then you will hear from heaven, and you will forgive my sins. God, you bless those who realize their need for you, for the kingdom of heaven is given to them. I will be very glad, for a great reward awaits me in heaven. Jesus says, "There are many rooms in my Father's home, and I am going to prepare a place for you. When everything is ready, I will come and get you, so that you will always be with me where I am."

SCRIPTURE REFERENCES

Jude 21
John 3:16
Romans 10:9
Romans 2:7
Isaiah 26:4
Romans 5:11
2 Corinthians 9:15
2 Chronicles 7:14
Matthew 5:3
Matthew 5:12
John 14:2, 3

FAITH

God, I pray I will strip off every weight that slows me down, especially the sin that so easily hinders my progress. And let me run with endurance the race that you have set before me. I will do this by keeping my eyes on Jesus, on whom my faith depends, from start to finish. He was willing to die a shameful death on the cross, because of the joy he knew would be his afterward. Now he is seated in the place of highest honor beside your throne in heaven. I need to fight the good fight, finish the race, and remain faithful. Then a prize awaits me—the crown of righteousness that you, Lord, the righteous Judge, will give me on that great day of your return. For if I am faithful to the end, and trust you, God, just as firmly as when I first believed, I will share in all that belongs to Christ. I pray I will let my roots grow down into Jesus and draw up nourishment from him, so I will grow in faith, strong and vigorous in the truth I have been taught. Oh, how kind and gracious you are. You have filled me completely with faith and the love of Jesus.

SCRIPTURE
REFERENCES

Hebrews 12:1, 2
2 Timothy 4:7, 8
Hebrews 3:14
Colossians 2:7
1 Timothy 1:14

FORGIVENESS

God, I pray you will have mercy on me, because of your unfailing love. Because of your great compassion, blot out the stain of my sins. Wash me clean from my guilt. Purify me from my sins, and I will be clean. Wash me, and I will be whiter than snow. Create in me a clean heart, O God. Renew a right spirit within me. The sacrifice you want is a broken spirit—a broken and repentant heart. I am deeply sorry for what I have done. Restore to me again the joy of my salvation, and make me willing to obey you. I have hidden your word in my heart that I might not sin against you. Grant me purity of heart, that I may honor you. With all my heart I praise you, O Lord, my God. You forgive me; all my guilt is gone. You are so good, so ready to forgive, so full of unfailing love for all who ask your aid. You blot out my sins for your own sake and will never think of them again. How gracious and merciful you are. I thank you, Lord, with all my heart.

SCRIPTURE REFERENCES

Psalm 51:1, 2
Psalm 51:7
Psalm 51:10
Psalm 51:17
Psalm 38:18
Psalm 51:12
Psalm 119:11
Psalm 86:11, 12
Psalm 32:5
Psalm 86:5
Isaiah 43:25
Psalm 111:4
Psalm 111:1

GOD CARES

God, I pray I will confidently trust in you to care for me. You have created me and cared for me since before I was born. You have examined my heart and know everything about me. You know when I sit down or stand up. You know my every thought when far away. You chart my path ahead of me and tell me where to stop and rest. Every moment you know where I am. You know what I am going to say, even before I say it. You place your hand of blessing on my head. You made all the delicate inner parts of my body and knit me together in my mother's womb! You saw me before I was born. Every day of my life was recorded in your book. Every moment was laid out before a single day had passed. How precious are your thoughts about me, O God! Your love for me is great. You surround me with love and tender mercies and you fill my life with good things. I thank you, Lord, with all my heart. I will give all my worries and cares to you. For you care about what happens to me. You alone are my rock and my salvation, my fortress where I will not be shaken.

SCRIPTURE REFERENCES

Psalm 112:7
Isaiah 46:3
Psalm 139:1–5
Psalm 139:13
Psalm 139:16, 17
Psalm 86:13
Psalm 103:4, 5
Psalm 111:1
1 Peter 5:7
Psalm 62:6

GODLINESS

God, I pray I will pursue godliness. For you bless the godly, surrounding them with your shield of love. I can be sure of this; you have set apart the godly for yourself and you will answer me when I call you. You protect the lives of your godly people and rescue them from the power of the wicked. You shower me with blessings. I will rejoice and be glad in your presence, and I will be filled with joy. For you offer your friendship to the godly. You grant a treasure of good sense, and you are my shield, protecting those who walk with integrity. I pray you will direct my steps for you delight in every detail in my life. You will never abandon me. You will keep me safe forever. The gateway to heaven leads to the presence of you, my God, and the godly enter there. I thank you for answering my prayer and saving me! I praise your holy name. For the hopes of the godly will come true and result in joy. I fill my heart with your laws, so I will never slip from your path. Though I may stumble, I will not fall, for you hold me by your hand.

SCRIPTURE REFERENCES

Proverbs 15:9
Psalm 5:12
Psalm 4:3
Psalm 97:10
Proverbs 10:6
Psalm 68:3
Proverbs 3:32
Proverbs 2:7
Psalm 37:23
Psalm 37:28
Genesis 28:17
Psalm 118:20, 21
Psalm 97:12
Proverbs 10:24
Proverbs 10:28
Psalm 37:31
Psalm 37:24

GOD'S WILL

God, I pray I will trust in you with all my heart, and not depend on my own understanding. I need to seek your will in all I do, and you will direct my paths. When I need wisdom—if I want to know what you want me to do—I will ask you, and you will gladly tell me. You will not resent me asking. But when I ask you, I need to be sure that I really expect you to answer me. For you say, "I will guide you along the best pathway for your life. I will advise you and watch over you." And you will hear my voice say, "This is the way, turn around and walk here." Your word is a lamp to my feet and a light for my path. I need to study your word continually and meditate on it day and night so I may be sure to obey all that is written in it. Only then will I succeed. I pray I will not copy the behavior and customs of this world, but that I would let you transform me into a new person by changing the way I think. Then I will know what you want me to do, and I will know how good and pleasing and perfect your will really is. For the steps of the godly are directed by you. I will praise your name forever and ever, for you alone have all wisdom and power. You are most worthy of praise!

SCRIPTURE REFERENCES

Proverbs 3:5, 6
James 1:5
Psalm 32:8
Isaiah 30:21
Psalm 119:105
Joshua 1:8
Romans 12:2
Psalm 37:23
Daniel 2:20
Psalm 145:3

GOD'S LOVE

God, I pray I will have the power to understand, as all God's people should, how wide, how long, how high, and how deep your love really is. May I experience the love of Christ, though it is so great I will never fully understand it. Then I will be filled with the fullness of life and power that comes from you. For you lavish your love on those who love you and obey you. You are my loving ally and my fortress, my tower of safety, my deliverer. I take refuge in you. Your loved ones are precious to you. You will work out your plans for my life, for your faithful love endures forever. For you so loved the world that you gave your only Son, so that everyone who believes in him will not perish but have eternal life. For you, my Father, love me dearly, because I love Jesus and believe that he came from you. Thank you, Lord, for still waiting for me to come to you, so you can show me your love and compassion. Your unfailing love is better to me than life itself. How I praise you.

SCRIPTURE REFERENCES

Ephesians 3:18, 19
Exodus 20:6
Psalm 144:2
Psalm 116:15
Psalm 138:8
John 3:16
John 16:27
Isaiah 30:18
Psalm 63:3

GOD'S WORD

God, I pray I will turn my eyes from worthless things, and that you will give me life through your word, for your word is full of living power. It is sharper than the sharpest knife, cutting deep into my innermost thoughts and desires. It exposes me for what I really am. Nothing in all creation can hide from you. Everything is naked and exposed before your eyes. You are the God to whom I must explain all that I have done. I pray I will hide your word in my heart, that I might not sin against you. That I may live and obey your word. Lord, I promise to obey your words! I used to wander off until you disciplined me; but now I closely follow your word. The suffering you sent was good for me, for it taught me to pay attention to your principles. How sweet are your words to my taste; they are sweeter than honey. I faint with longing for your salvation; I have put my hope in your word. My lips burst forth with praise to you, my God. Your promises revive me.

SCRIPTURE REFERENCES

Psalm 119:37
Hebrews 4:12, 13
Psalm 119:11
Psalm 119:17
Psalm 119:57
Psalm 119:67
Psalm 119:71
Psalm 119:103
Psalm 119:81
Psalm 119:171
Psalm 119:50

GUIDANCE

God, I pray you will guide me along the best pathway for my life, that you would advise me and watch over me and teach me good judgment and knowledge. Guide my steps by your word, so I will not be overcome by any evil. Your word is a lamp to my feet and a light for my path. Look down on me with your love; teach me all your principles. I pray my actions would consistently reflect your principles. How sweet are your words to my taste; they are sweeter than honey. I belong to you; you are holding my right hand. You will keep on guiding me with your counsel, leading me to a glorious destiny. I desire you more than anything on earth. Lord, you are mine! I promise to obey your words! I have hidden your word in my heart that I might not sin against you. Turn my eyes from worthless things, and give me life through your word. I need to make your commands my constant guide.

SCRIPTURE REFERENCES

Psalm 32:8
Psalm 119:66
Psalm 119:133
Psalm 119:105
Psalm 119:135
Psalm 119:5
Psalm 119:103
Psalm 73:23–25
Psalm 119:57
Psalm 119:11
Psalm 119:37
Psalm 119:98

HEARTS

God, I pray that the words of my mouth and the thoughts of my heart would be pleasing to you, O Lord, my rock and redeemer. I know that you examine my heart and rejoice when you find integrity there. For you look deep within the mind and heart. Grant me purity of heart, that I may honor you. For you bless those whose hearts are pure, for they will see you. If I will search for you with all my heart and soul, I will find you. I want to go right into your presence, with a true heart, and fully trusting you. I pray I will keep away from anything that might take your place in my heart. With all my heart I praise you. Your decrees are my treasures; they are truly my heart's delight. I will give glory to your name forever. I love you with all my heart, all my soul, and all my mind. You will delight in me if I obey your voice, keep your commands, and turn to you with all my heart and soul.

SCRIPTURE REFERENCES

Psalm 19:14

1 Chronicles 29:17

Psalm 7:9

Psalm 86:11

Matthew 5:8

Deuteronomy 4:29

Hebrews 10:22

1 John 5:21

Psalm 86:12

Psalm 119:111

Psalm 86:12

Matthew 22:37

Deuteronomy 30:10

HOLY

God, I pray I will keep myself pure, and then I will be an instrument you can use for your purposes. My life will be clean, and I will be ready for you to use me for every good work. I need to let your light so shine before men, that they may see your good works and glorify you, my heavenly Father. May you, the God of peace, make me holy in every way, and may my whole spirit, soul, and body be kept blameless until that day when my Lord Jesus Christ comes again. Since everything around me is going to melt away, what a holy, godly life I should be living! Now I am free from the power of sin and have become a slave to you. Now I do those things that lead to holiness and result in eternal life. For you, the Mighty One, are holy and have done great things for me. In you my heart rejoices, for I am trusting in your holy name. I pray I will try to live in peace with everyone, and seek to live a clean and holy life, for those who are not holy will not see you. I must be holy in everything I do, just as you, God, who chose me to be your child, is holy. For you have said, "You must be holy because I am holy."

SCRIPTURE REFERENCES

2 Timothy 2:21 NLT, NIV
Matthew 5:16 NKJ
1 Thessalonians 5:23
2 Peter 3:11
Romans 6:22
Luke 1:49
Psalm 33:21
Hebrews 12:14
1 Peter 1:15, 16

HOLY SPIRIT

God, I pray I will let the Holy Spirit fill and control me, for you have given me your Spirit as proof that I live in you and you in me. My body is the temple of the Holy Spirit, who lives in me and was given to me by you. Your Spirit speaks to me deep in my heart and tells me that I am your child. When the Holy Spirit controls my life, he will produce this kind of fruit in me: love, joy, peace, patience, kindness, goodness, faithfulness, gentleness, and self-control. I pray I will live according to my new life in the Holy Spirit. Then I won't be doing what my sinful nature craves. The old sinful nature loves to do evil, which is opposite from what the Holy Spirit wants. And the Holy Spirit gives me desires that are opposite from what the sinful nature desires. These two forces are constantly fighting each other, and my choices are never free from conflict. But the Spirit helps me in my weakness, because the Spirit intercedes for me in accordance with your will. And the Holy Spirit gives me more and more strength to stand against evil desires, because he jealously longs for me to be faithful. I need to follow the Holy Spirit's leading in every part of my life; so that I do not bring sorrow to the Holy Spirit by the way I live. I thank you and praise your glorious name for filling me with your Spirit that gives me new life from heaven.

SCRIPTURE REFERENCES

Ephesians 5:18
1 John 4:13
1 Corinthians 6:19
Romans 8:16
Galatians 5:22, 23
Galatians 5:16, 17
Romans 8:26, 27 NIV
James 4:5, 6
Galatians 5:25
Ephesians 4:30
1 Chronicles 29:13
John 3:6

HOPE

God, I pray I will trust in you, and that I will put my hope and confidence in you. For your delight is in me when I honor you and put my hope in your unfailing love. Let your unfailing love surround me, for my hope is in you alone. You faithfully answer my prayers with awesome deeds. When doubts filled my mind, your comfort gave me renewed hope and cheer. For you know the plans you have for me. "They are plans for good and not for disaster, to give me a future and a hope." You who began a good work within me will continue your work, until it is finished on the day when Christ Jesus comes back again. I pray you will keep me joyful and full of peace, as I believe in you. May I overflow with hope through the power of the Holy Spirit. My body rests in hope. You have shown me the way of life, and you will give me wonderful joy in your presence. I praise you, my God and King, and I will bless your name forever and ever.

SCRIPTURE REFERENCES

Jeremiah 17:7
Psalm 147:11
Psalm 33:22
Psalm 65:5
Psalm 94:19
Jeremiah 29:11
Philippians 1:6
Romans 15:13 NLT, NIV
Acts 2:26
Acts 2:28
Psalm 145:1

HUSBANDS

God, I pray I will love my wife with the same love Christ showed the church. He gave up his life for her. May I always be captivated by her love and be faithful to her. A man who finds a wife finds a treasure and receives favor from you, Lord. I must give honor to her and treat her with understanding as we live together. If I don't treat her as I should, my prayers will not be heard. For you, Lord, see clearly what I do, examining every path I take. I need to fear you and turn my back on evil. There must be no sexual immorality, impurity, or greed in my life. Such sins have no place among your people. Jesus, you teach us that anyone who even looks at a woman with lust in his eyes has already committed adultery with her in his heart. So I need to guard my heart, for it affects everything I do. I will share my love only with my wife and love her as I love my own body. I pray I will be careful to live a blameless life and lead a life of integrity in my home. May we submit to one another in our marriage. O Lord, I do honor and praise your name, for you are my God. You do such wonderful things!

SCRIPTURE REFERENCES

Ephesians 5:25

Proverbs 5:19

1 Timothy 3:2

Proverbs 18:22

1 Peter 3:7

Proverbs 5:21

Proverbs 3:7

Ephesians 5:3

Matthew 5:28

Proverbs 4:23

Proverbs 5:15

Ephesians 5:28

Psalm 101:2

Ephesians 5:21

Isaiah 25:1

INTEGRITY

God, I pray I will act with integrity and trust you without wavering. I know that you examine my heart and rejoice when you find integrity there. I must act in the fear of you; with integrity and with an undivided heart. Teach me your ways, that I may live according to your truth. Grant me purity of heart that I may honor you. I pray I will fix my thoughts on what is true and honorable and right; that I will reject perverse ideas and stay away from every evil. I want to live honorably in everything I do. I need to clothe myself with tenderhearted mercy, kindness, humility, gentleness, and patience. Since I have been raised to a new life with Christ, I will set my sights on the realities of heaven, where Christ sits at the right hand in the place of honor and power. May heaven fill my thoughts, and not only things down here on earth. Turn my eyes from worthless things and keep me working toward that day when I will finally be all that Christ Jesus saved me for and wants me to be. I need to focus all my energies on this one thing: forgetting the past and looking to what lies ahead. I will strain to reach the end of the race and win the prize for which you, God, have called me heavenward in Christ Jesus. I am a citizen of heaven, and I will have the pleasures of living with you forever. With all my heart I praise you; I will give glory to your name forever.

SCRIPTURE REFERENCES

Psalm 26:1

1 Chronicles 29:17

2 Chronicles 19:9

Psalm 86:11

Philippians 4:8

Psalm 101:4

Hebrews 13:18

Colossians 3:12

Colossians 3:1, 2

Psalm 119:37

Philippians 3:12–14 NLT, NIV

Philippians 3:20

Psalm 16:11

Psalm 86:12

JOY

Good, I pray you will show me the way of life, granting me the joy of your presence and the pleasures of living with you forever. Yes, what joy for those whose record you have cleared of sin. I take joy in doing your will, my God, for your law is written on my heart. Your words are what sustain me. They bring me great joy and are my heart's delight, for I bear your name, O Lord God Almighty. I think how much you have helped me. I sing for joy in the shadow of your protecting wings. I follow close behind you; your strong right hand holds me securely. Those who look to you for help will be radiant with joy. I pray that I will search for you and be filled with joy and gladness. You will fill my mouth with laughter and my lips with shouts of joy, so I will rejoice in you and be glad. Oh, the joys of those who trust in you. You fill my life with good things. I praise you and give thanks to you, my Lord, for you are good! Your faithful love endures forever.

SCRIPTURE REFERENCES

Psalm 16:11
Psalm 32:2
Psalm 40:8
Jeremiah 15:16
Psalm 63:7, 8
Psalm 34:5
Psalm 40:16
Job 8:21
Psalm 32:11
Psalm 40:4
Psalm 103:5
Psalm 106:1

LUKEWARM SPIRITUALLY

God, I pray I will return to you, and you will return to me. I have wandered away like a lost sheep; come and find me. God, I know my deeds are far from right in your sight. I need to go back to what I heard and believed at first, and hold on to it firmly, and turn to you again. For God, you have said, "I know all the things that you do, that you are neither hot nor cold. I wish you were one or the other! But since you are like lukewarm water, I will spit you out of my mouth! I am the one who corrects and disciplines everyone I love. Be diligent and turn from your indifference. For I have one complaint against you. You don't love me as you did at first. Look how far you have fallen from your first love!" God, I know you know the secrets of my heart. I confess my sins to you. You are faithful and just to forgive me and cleanse me from every wrong. I need to be careful to make sure that my own heart is not evil and unbelieving, turning me away from you. I pray I will not be deceived by sin and harden myself against you. For if I am faithful to the end, trusting you just as firmly as when I first believed, I will share in all that belongs to Christ. I praise you, my God and King. For you are most worthy of my praise!

SCRIPTURE REFERENCES

Malachi 3:7

Psalm 119:176

Revelation 3:2, 3

Revelation 3:15, 16

Revelation 3:19

Revelation 2:4, 5

Psalm 44:21

1 John 1:9

Hebrews 3:12–14

Psalm 145:1

Psalm 145:3

MARRIAGE

God, I pray we will submit to one another out of reverence for Christ. You made us male and female and the two of us are united as one. Since we are no longer two but one, let no one separate us, for you have joined us together. For you said, "It is not good for a man to be alone. I will make a companion who will help him." God you teach us that a husband must love his wife with the same love Christ showed the church. He gave up his life for her. Wives are to submit to their husbands as they do to you, Lord. Each man must love his wife as he loves himself, and the wife must respect her husband. Love is patient and kind. Love is not jealous or boastful or proud or rude. Love does not demand its own way. Love is not irritable, and keeps no record of when it has been wronged. It is never glad about injustice but rejoices whenever the truth wins out. Love never gives up, never loses faith, is always hopeful, and endures through every circumstance. I pray our love for each other will last forever and that we will love each other intensely with all our hearts. That we will not sin by letting anger gain control over us. We need to not let the sun go down while we are still angry, for anger gives a mighty foothold to the devil. We need to honor you in our marriage, and remain faithful to one another. I pray we will serve you wholeheartedly together and that we will bless your name forever and ever.

SCRIPTURE REFERENCES

Ephesians 5:21

Matthew 19:4–6

Genesis 2:18

Ephesians 5:25

Ephesians 5:22

Ephesians 5:33

1 Corinthians 13:4–8

1 Peter 1:22

Ephesians 4:26, 27

Hebrews 13:4

Joshua 24:14

Psalm 145:2

NATION

God, I pray for our president and all our leaders who are in authority, that we might live in peace and quietness, in godliness and dignity. This is good and pleases you, for you want everyone to be saved and to understand the truth. I ask you to make our leaders wise with spiritual wisdom and give them complete understanding of what you want them to do with our nation. Then our nation will always honor and please you. Without wise leadership, a nation falls. When there is moral rot within a nation, its government topples easily. But with wise and knowledgeable leaders, there is stability. When we obey all the laws you gave us, and do not turn away from them, we will be successful in everything we do. I pray the people of our nation will turn from their wicked deeds. Let them banish from their minds the very thought of doing wrong! Let them turn to you, God, that you may have mercy on them. In every nation you accept those who fear you and do what is right. May blessings rest on your people. Please rescue us from our enemies. Protect us from those who are trying to destroy us. May all nations praise you and recognize that you are glorious and strong.

SCRIPTURE REFERENCES

1 Timothy 2:1–3
Colossians 1:9, 10
Proverbs 11:14
Proverbs 28:2
Joshua 1:7
Isaiah 55:7
Acts 10:35
Psalm 3:8
Psalm 59:1
Psalm 67:3
Psalm 96:7

OBEDIENCE

God, I pray you will put your laws in my heart so I will understand them, and write them on my mind so I will obey them. You are working in me, giving me the desire to obey you and the power to do what pleases you. You bless me when I keep your statutes and seek you with all my heart. You lavish your love on those who love you and obey your commands. Lord, I love to obey your laws; my heart's desire is to glorify your name. Those who obey your word really do love you. You will lead me with unfailing love and faithfulness when I keep your covenant and obey your decrees. I pray I will guard your teachings as my most precious possession and write them deep within my heart. You delight in me if I obey your voice and keep your commands, and if I turn to you with all my heart and soul. I pray I will obey your commandments and live in fellowship with you. And I know you live in me, because the Holy Spirit lives in me. I praise you from the bottom of my heart.

SCRIPTURE
REFERENCES

Hebrews 10:16

Philippians 2:13

Psalm 119:2 NIV

Exodus 20:6

Isaiah 26:8

1 John 2:5

Psalm 25:10

Proverbs 7:2, 3

Deuteronomy 30:10

1 John 3:24

Psalm 35:10

ORPHANS AND WIDOWS

God, I pray you will turn to me and have mercy on me, for I am alone and in deep distress. Feel my pain and see my trouble. For you care for the orphans and widows. God, you are a father to the fatherless, a defender of widows. You know the hopes of the helpless. You listen to my cries and comfort me. You give power to me when I am tired and worn out; you offer strength when I am weak. You will bring justice to the orphans and the oppressed, so people can no longer terrify them. You will help the oppressed, who have no one to defend them. I know you are always with me. I will not be shaken, for you are right beside me. My life is precious to you. I give all my worries and cares to you, for you care about what happens to me. You are my loving ally and fortress, my tower of safety and my deliverer. You are my refuge from the storm. When I am needy in distress, you are my shelter. You tell me, "Don't be afraid, for I am with you. Do not be dismayed, for I am your God. I will strengthen you. I will help you." I pray I won't be afraid, for I am deeply loved by you. I will trust in you with all my heart. I praise you from the bottom of my heart.

SCRIPTURE REFERENCES

Psalm 25:16
Psalm 25:18
Psalm 146:9
Psalm 68:5
Psalm 10:17
Isaiah 40:29
Psalm 10:18
Psalm 72:12
Psalm 16:8
Psalm 72:14
1 Peter 5:7
Psalm 144:2
Isaiah 25:4
Isaiah 41:10
Daniel 10:19
Proverbs 3:5
Psalm 35:10

PEACE

God, I pray I will not worry about anything, but instead pray about everything. That I would tell you what I need and thank you for all you have done. When I do this, I will experience your peace, which is far more wonderful than the human mind can understand. Your peace will guard my heart and mind as I live in Christ Jesus. You will bless me with your special favor and wonderful peace, as I come to know Jesus my Lord better and better. I need to let the peace that comes from Christ rule in my heart. Jesus said, "He was leaving me a gift: peace of mind and heart. And that the peace he gives isn't like the peace the world gives. So I shouldn't be troubled or afraid." Lord you are my shepherd, I have everything I need. You let me rest in green meadows; you lead me beside peaceful streams. You renew my strength; you guide me along right paths, bringing honor to your name. You watch over the sheep under your care. Those who love your law have great peace and do not stumble. I rejoice in your word like one who finds a great treasure. I praise your holy name with my whole heart, and I will never forget the good things you have done for me. You ransomed me from death and surround me with your love and tender mercies.

SCRIPTURE REFERENCES

Philippians 4:6, 7
2 Peter 1:2
Colossians 3:15
John 14:27
Psalm 23:1–3
Psalm 95:7
Psalm 119:165
Psalm 119:162
Psalm 103:1, 2
Psalm 103:4

PLEASING GOD

God, I pray that you will give me complete understanding of what you want me to do in my life, and that you would make me wise with spiritual wisdom. Then the way I live will always honor and please you, and I will continually do good, kind things for others. All the while I will learn to know you better and better. I pray I will be strengthened with your glorious power, so that I will have all the patience and endurance I need. I need to let you transform me into a new person by changing the way I think. Then I will know what you want me to do, and I will know how good and pleasing and perfect your will really is. May you produce in me, through the power of Jesus Christ, all that is pleasing to you. May you be pleased by all my thoughts about you, for I rejoice in you, my Lord. I will praise your name forever and ever, for you alone have all wisdom and power. You give wisdom, knowledge, and joy to those who please you. I thank you and praise your glorious name!

SCRIPTURE REFERENCES

Colossians 1:9–11

Romans 12:2

Hebrews 13:21

Psalm 104:34

Daniel 2:20

Ecclesiastes 2:26

1 Chronicles 29:13

PRAISE AND WORSHIP

God, I pray I will bless you everyday, and that I will praise you forever. I exalt your holy name, O Lord; the majesty of your name fills the earth! Your glory is higher than the heavens. I worship you at your throne—eternal, high, and glorious! The one thing I ask of you, Lord, the thing I seek most, is to live in your house all the days of my life, delighting in your perfections and meditating in your temple. I pray that you will show me the way of life, granting me the joy of your presence and the pleasures of living with you forever. Please let me see your glorious presence. Blessed are those who hear the joyful call to worship you, for they will walk in the light of your presence. I worship you Lord in the splendor of your holiness. I will honor you and serve you wholeheartedly. With my whole heart, I praise your holy name. You are my God; you do such wonderful things! You love me with unfailing love and your faithfulness endures forever. I thank you with all my heart.

SCRIPTURE
REFERENCES

Psalm 145:2

Psalm 105:3

Psalm 8:1

Jeremiah 17:12

Psalm 27:4

Psalm 16:11

Exodus 33:18

Psalm 89:15 NIV, NLT

Psalm 29:2

Joshua 24:14

Psalm 103:1

Isaiah 25:1

Psalm 117:2

Psalm 111:1

PRAYER

God, I pray I will not worry about anything; instead that I would pray about everything. That I would tell you what I need and thank you for all you have done. If I do this, I will experience your peace, which is far more wonderful than the human mind can understand. Your peace will guard my heart and mind as I live in Jesus Christ. I need to pray at all times and on every occasion in the power of the Holy Spirit. And to stay alert and be persistent in my prayers for all Christians everywhere. You desire that I pray for all people. As I make requests, I need to plead for your mercy upon them, and give thanks. I need to pray this way for kings and all others who are in authority, so we can live in peace and quietness, in godliness and dignity. This is good and pleasing to you, for you want everyone to be saved and to understand the truth. You faithfully answer my prayers with awesome deeds. I love you, Lord, because you hear and answer my prayers. I need to keep alert and pray. Otherwise temptation will overpower me. For though the spirit is willing enough, the body is weak. When I pray, you answer me; you encourage me by giving me the strength I need. You delight in the prayers of the upright.

SCRIPTURE REFERENCES

Philippians 4:6
Ephesians 6:18
1 Timothy 2:1–4
Psalm 65:5
Psalm 116:1
Matthew 26:41
Psalm 138:3
Proverbs 15:8

PRAYING FOR MY CHILDREN

God, I pray my children will love you with all their heart, all their soul, and all their mind. That they will learn to be wise and develop good judgment. May you give them complete understanding of what you want them to do in their lives, and make them wise with spiritual wisdom. Then the way they live will always honor and please you, and they will continually do good, kind things for others. All the while they will learn to know you better and better. I thank you with all my heart for my children, for they are a gift from you; they are a reward. I need to bring them up with the discipline and instruction approved by you, to teach them to choose the right path, and when they are older, they will remain upon it. May they realize their need for you, for the kingdom of heaven will be given to them. I pray they will not do as the wicked do, or follow the path of evildoers. Lord, make them strong and guard them from the evil one. For every child of yours defeats this evil world by trusting Christ to give the victory. And the ones who win this battle against the world are the ones who believe that Jesus is the Son of God. I pray my children will cling to Jesus and never stop trusting him. O Lord, I do honor and praise your name, for you are my God. You do such wonderful things!

SCRIPTURE REFERENCES

Matthew 22:37

Proverbs 4:5

Colossians 1:9–11

Psalm 111:1

Psalm 127:3

Ephesians 6:4

Proverbs 22:6

Matthew 5:3

Proverbs 4:14

2 Thessalonians 3:3

1 John 5:4, 5

Hebrews 4:14

Isaiah 25:1

PRAYING FOR MY HUSBAND

God, I pray my husband will love you with all his heart, all his soul, and all his strength. That he would not compromise with evil, and walk only on your path. May he be careful to live a blameless life, follow the steps of good men, and stay on the path of the righteous. May integrity and honesty protect him. I pray he will love me deeply, from the heart. That he will guard himself and remain loyal to me. The marriage bed must be kept pure, for you, God, will judge the adulterer, and all the sexually immoral. Let us cleanse ourselves from everything that can defile our body or spirit. And let us work toward complete purity because we fear you. We need to hide your word in our hearts that we might not sin against you. We need to be humble and gentle with each other. And be patient, making allowances for each other's faults, because of your love for us. May we keep ourselves united in the Holy Spirit, and bind ourselves together with peace. In you our hearts rejoice, for we trust in your holy name.

SCRIPTURE REFERENCES

Deuteronomy 6:5

Psalm 119:3

Psalm 101:2

Proverbs 2:20

Psalm 25:21

1 Peter 1:22 NIV

Malachi 2:16

Hebrews 13:4 NIV

2 Corinthians 7:1

Psalm 119:11

Ephesians 4:2

Psalm 33:21

PRAYING FOR MY WIFE

God, I pray my wife will be known for her beauty that comes from within—the unfading beauty of a gentle and quiet spirit, which is so precious to you. May she commit her way to you and trust in you so that you will make your righteousness shine like the dawn. May she be righteous in your eyes and be careful to obey all your commandments. May she be an example to all believers in what she teaches, in the way she lives, in her love, her faith, and her purity. I pray she will submit to me as she does to you, God, and that I will love her and never treat her harshly. We need to allow the Holy Spirit to control our lives; when we do he will produce this kind of fruit in us: love, joy, peace, patience, kindness, goodness, faithfulness, gentleness, and self-control. Let us not become conceited, or irritate one another. We need to really love each other intensely with all our hearts. May you produce in us, through the power of Jesus Christ, all that is pleasing to you. I give thanks to you and praise your glorious name!

SCRIPTURE REFERENCES

1 Peter 3:4

Psalm 37:5, 6 NIV

Luke 1:6

1 Timothy 4:12

Ephesians 5:22

Colossians 3:19

Galatians 5:22, 23

1 Thessalonians 2:17

1 Peter 1:22

Hebrews 13:21

1 Chronicles 29:13

PROTECTION

God, I pray I will live in the shelter of the Most High and find rest in the Shadow of you, the Almighty. You alone are my refuge, my place of safety. You are my God, and I am trusting you. I think how much you have helped me. I sing for joy in the shadow of your protecting wings. I follow close behind you; your strong right hand holds me securely. Lord, you say, "I will rescue those who love me. I will protect those who trust in my name. When they call on me, I will answer. I will be with them in trouble. I will rescue them and honor them." I love you, Lord, you are my strength. You are my rock, my fortress, and my Savior, in whom I find protection. You are my hiding place; you protect me from trouble. You surround me with songs of victory. You say, "I will guide you along the best pathway for your life. I will advise you and watch over you." You grant a treasure of good sense to the godly. You are their shield, protecting those who walk with integrity. You guard the paths of justice and protect those who are faithful to you. How good it is to be near you, God! I pray I will make you my shelter and that I will tell everyone about the wonderful things you do.

SCRIPTURE
REFERENCES

Psalm 91:1, 2
Psalm 63:7, 8
Psalm 91:14, 15
Psalm 18:1
Psalm 32:7, 8
Proverbs 2:7, 8
Psalm 73:28

SALVATION

God, I pray you will open my eyes, so I may turn from darkness to light, and from the power of Satan to you. Then I will receive forgiveness for my sins and be given a place among your people, who are set apart by faith in Jesus Christ. For if I confess with my mouth that Jesus is Lord, and believe in my heart that you raised him from the dead, I will be saved. For it is by believing in my heart that I am made right with you, and it is by confessing with my mouth that I am saved. God, you paid a ransom to save me from the empty life I inherited from my ancestors. And the ransom you paid was not mere gold or silver. You paid for me with the precious life blood of Christ, the sinless, spotless Lamb. For you so loved the world that you gave your only Son, so that everyone who believes in him will not perish but have eternal life. I pray you will show me your unfailing love and grant me your salvation and the forgiveness of my sins. Wash me clean from my guilt. Purify me from my sin. I thank you for answering my prayer and saving me! I praise you from the bottom of my heart.

SCRIPTURE REFERENCES

Acts 26:18
Romans 10:9, 10
1 Peter 1:18, 19
John 3:16
Psalm 85:7
Matthew 6:12
Psalm 51:2
Psalm 118:21
Psalm 35:10

SALVATION FOR EVERYONE

God, I pray for the entire world to look to you for salvation. For you are God; there is no other. There is salvation in no one else! There is no other name in all of heaven for people to call to save them. You desire that I pray for all people. As I make requests, I need to plead for your mercy upon them, and give thanks. I need to pray this way for kings and all others who are in authority, so we can live in peace and quietness, in godliness and dignity. This is good and pleases you, for you want everyone to be saved and to understand the truth. The truth is that there is only one God and one Mediator who can reconcile God and people. He is the man of Christ Jesus. He gave his life to purchase freedom for everyone. I pray for all people, that you will open their eyes so they may turn from darkness to light and from the power of Satan to you. For you so loved the world that you gave your only Son, so that everyone who believes in him will not perish but have eternal life. For anyone who calls on the name of the Lord will be saved. For Christ came into the world to save sinners. If they look for you in earnest, they will find you when you seek you. May they seek first your kingdom and your righteousness. Show them your unfailing love and grant them your salvation. I thank you and praise your glorious name!

SCRIPTURE REFERENCES

Isaiah 45:22

Acts 4:12

1 Timothy 2:1–6

Acts 26:18

John 3:16

Romans 10:13

1 Timothy 1:15

Jeremiah 29:13

Matthew 6:33 NIV

Psalm 85:7

1 Chronicles 29:13

SALVATION FOR FAMILY AND FRIENDS

God, I pray you will open the eyes of (names) so they may turn from darkness to light and from the power of Satan to you. Then they will receive forgiveness for their sins and be given a place among your people, who are set apart by faith in Jesus Christ. For you so loved the world that you gave your only Son, so that everyone who believes in him will not perish but have eternal life. For anyone who calls on the name of the Lord will be saved. I pray they will confess with their mouth that Jesus is Lord and believe in their heart that you raised him from the dead, and then they will be saved. That they would seek you, Lord, while you may be found, and call on you while you are near, and turn from their wicked deeds. Let them banish from their mind the very thought of doing wrong. Let them turn to you, that you would have mercy on them. Yes, they will turn to you, for you will abundantly pardon them. Show them your unfailing love and grant them your salvation. For you want everyone to be saved and to understand the truth. How gracious and merciful you are. Your goodness is so great. I thank you with all my heart!

SCRIPTURE REFERENCES

Acts 26:18

John 3:16

Romans 10:13

Romans 10:9

Isaiah 55:6, 7

Psalm 85:7

1 Timothy 2:3

Psalm 111:4

Psalm 31:19

Psalm 111:1

SATAN DEFEATED

God, I pray I will be careful and watch out for attacks from Satan, my great enemy. For he prowls around like a roaring lion, looking for some victim to devour. I need to take a firm stand against him, and be strong in my faith. Lord you are faithful; you will make me strong and guard me from the evil one. I will humble myself before you. I will resist the devil, and he will flee from me. I will draw close to you, and you will draw close to me. You have rescued me from the one who rules in the kingdom of darkness, and you have brought me into the kingdom of your dear Son. I pray I will live in this evil world with self-control, right conduct, and devotion to you. How great you are, Lord! Your power is absolute. I will be strong with your mighty power. I need to put on all of your armor so that I will be able to stand firm against all strategies and tricks of the devil. I have hidden your word in my heart that I might not sin against you. Because I am strong with your word living in my heart, I have won my battle with Satan. I thank you with all my heart.

SCRIPTURE
REFERENCES

1 Peter 5:8, 9
2 Thessalonians 3:3
James 4:7, 8
Colossians 1:13
Titus 2:12
Psalm 147:5
Ephesians 6:10, 11
Psalm 119:11
1 John 2:14
Psalm 111:1

SEEKING GOD

God, I pray I will seek first your kingdom and your righteousness. You are my God, I earnestly search for you. My soul thirsts for you, my whole body longs for you in this parched and weary land where there is no water. As the deer pants for streams of water, so I long for you. Jesus said, "I am the bread of life. No one who comes to me will ever be hungry again. Those who believe in me will never thirst." If I search for you with all my heart and soul, I will find you. God you say, "I know the plans I have for you. They are plans for good and not for disaster, to give you a future and a hope. When you pray, I will listen. If you look for me in earnest, you will find me when you seek me." I do seek you Lord and praise you. My heart rejoices with everlasting joy. I am blessed when I obey your decrees and search for you with all my heart, and do not compromise with evil. I pray I will walk only in your paths. Lord you are wonderfully good to those who wait for you and seek you.

SCRIPTURE REFERENCES

Matthew 6:33 NIV
Psalm 63:1
Psalm 42:1
John 6:35
Deuteronomy 4:29
Jeremiah 29:11–13
Psalm 22:26
Psalm 119:2, 3 NLT, NIV
Lamentations 3:25

SEXUAL IMMORALITY

God, I pray I will run away from sexual sin. No other sin so clearly affects the body as this one. For sexual immorality is a sin against my own body. My body is the temple of the Holy Spirit, who lives in me and was given to me by you. I do not belong to myself, for you bought me with a high price. So I must honor you with my body. I must run from anything that stimulates my lust and follow anything that makes me want to do right. I will pursue faith and love and peace, and enjoy the companionship of those who call on you with a pure heart. The human heart is most deceitful and desperately wicked. You search my heart and examine secret motives. You give all people their due rewards, according to their actions. I pray I will test and examine my ways, and turn again in repentance to you. I lift my heart and hands to you in heaven and say, "I have sinned and rebelled." God, I pour out my heart to you, for you are my refuge. I confess my sins to you, for you are faithful and just to forgive me and cleanse me from every wrong. You will keep my temptations from becoming so strong that I cannot stand up against them. When I am tempted, you will show me a way out, so that I will not give in to it. I put my trust in you, my hope and confidence. For I can do everything with the help of Christ who gives me the strength I need. I praise you Lord, for you have shown me your unfailing love.

SCRIPTURE REFERENCES

1 Corinthians 6:18–20

2 Timothy 2:22

Jeremiah 17:9, 10

Lamentations 3:40–42

Psalm 62:8

1 John 1:9

1 Corinthians 10:13

Jeremiah 17:7

Philippians 4:13

Psalm 31:21

SICKNESS

God, I pray you will have compassion on me, for I am weak. I am suffering and in pain. Rescue me by your saving power. You alone can heal me and you can save me. God, you nurse me when I am sick, and you ease my pain and discomfort. You are my God who comforts me. Your eyes watch over those who do right; your ears are open to their cries for help. I am crying out to you in my suffering and you have heard me. You have set me free from all my fears. I will not be afraid, for you are close beside me. I give all my worries and cares to you, for you care about what happens to me. Let your unfailing love surround me, for my hope is in you alone. Lord, you are my shepherd; I have everything I need. You let me rest in green meadows; you lead me beside peaceful streams. You renew my strength. You watch over the sheep under your care. I pray that I will be strong and take courage, for I can do everything with the help of Christ who gives me the strength I need. I will think of all the wonderful things you have done for me. I will praise your name forever and ever.

SCRIPTURE REFERENCES

Psalm 6:2
Psalm 69:29
Jeremiah 17:14
Psalm 41:3
2 Corinthians 1:4
Psalm 34:15
Psalm 34:6
Psalm 23:4
1 Peter 5:7
Psalm 33:22
Psalm 23:1–3
Psalm 95:7
Psalm 31:24
Philippians 4:13
1 Samuel 12:24
Daniel 2:20

SORROW

God, I pray I will not be dismayed, for you are my God. You will strengthen me and help me. You bless those who mourn, for they will be comforted. You give rest to the weary and joy to the sorrowing. I am overcome with joy because of your unfailing love, for you have seen my troubles, and you care about the anguish of my soul. You keep track of all my sorrows. You have collected all my tears in your bottle and have recorded each one in your book. Weeping may go on all night, but joy comes with the morning. You will give beauty for ashes, joy instead of mourning, and praise instead of despair. Jesus said, "Come to me, all of you who are weary and carry heavy burdens, and I will give you rest. Take my yoke upon you. Let me teach you, because I am humble and gentle, and you will find rest for your souls. For my yoke fits perfectly, and my burden I give you is light." I pray I will give all my worries and cares to you, Lord. For you care about what happens to me. I will sing to you, because you have been so good to me. I will rejoice, for you have rescued me, and you love me dearly.

SCRIPTURE REFERENCES

Isaiah 41:10

Matthew 5:4

Jeremiah 31:25

Psalm 31:7

Psalm 56:8

Psalm 30:5

Isaiah 61:3

Matthew 11:28–30

1 Peter 5:7

Psalm 13:6

Psalm 13:5

John 16:27

SPIRITUAL GROWTH

God, I pray you will give me spiritual wisdom and understanding, so that I might grow in my knowledge of you. May my heart be flooded with light, so I can understand the wonderful future you have promised to those you have called. Help me to realize what a rich and glorious inheritance you have given me. I want to understand what really matters, so that I will live a pure and blameless life until Christ returns. I must crave pure spiritual milk so that I can grow into the fullness of my salvation. I need to cry out for your nourishment as a baby cries for milk, now that I have had a taste of your kindness. God, you require me to fear you, to live according to your will, to love and worship you with all my heart and soul, and to obey your commands and laws. I pray that I will throw off my old evil nature and my former way of life, which is rotten through and through, full of lust and deception. Instead, there must be a spiritual renewal of my thoughts and attitudes. I must display a new nature because I am a new person, created in your likeness— righteous, holy, and true. I love and worship you with all my heart and soul. You are my great and awesome God!

SCRIPTURE REFERENCES

Ephesians 1:17, 18
Philippians 1:10
1 Peter 2:2, 3
Deuteronomy 10:12, 13
Ephesians 4:22–24
Deuteronomy 10:12
Daniel 9:4

STRENGTH

God, I pray your hand will guide me, and your strength will support me. You give power to those who are tired and worn out; you offer strength to the weak. You tell me to not be afraid, for you are with me and to not be dismayed, for you are my God. You will strengthen me. You will help me. You will uphold me with your victorious right hand. When I pray, you answer me; you encourage me by giving me the strength I need. Those who wait for you will find new strength. They will fly high on wings like eagles. They will run and not grow weary. They will walk and not faint. I have waited for you. Be my strength each day. Show me the wonder of your great love. You who save with your strength. Keep me as the apple of your eye; hide me in the shadow of your wings. I pray I will be strong and take courage, for I can do everything with the help of Christ who gives me the strength I need. I thank and praise you for you have given me wisdom and strength. You are my great and awesome God!

SCRIPTURE REFERENCES

Psalm 139:10
Isaiah 40:29
Isaiah 41:10
Psalm 138:3
Isaiah 40:31
Isaiah 33:2
Psalm 17:7, 8 NLT, NIV
Psalm 31:24
Philippians 4:13
Daniel 2:23
Daniel 9:4

SUFFERING

God, I pray I will trust in you at all times and that I will pour out my heart to you. For you do not turn away when I am suffering and in pain. But you hear my cry for help. You are my safe place in times of trouble. You tell me that after I have suffered a little while, you will restore, support, and strengthen me. Each day you carry me in your arms. I think how much you have helped me; I sing for joy in the shadow of your protection. I will follow close behind you; your strong right hand holds me securely. You are the strength of my heart; you are mine forever. I pray I will be truly glad for there is wonderful joy ahead, even though it is necessary for me to endure many trials for awhile. These trials are only to test my faith, to show that it is strong and pure. It is being tested as fire tests and purifies gold, and my faith is far more precious to you than mere gold. When my faith remains strong after being tried by fiery trials, it will bring me much praise and glory and honor on the day when Jesus Christ is revealed to the whole world. My reward for trusting Jesus Christ will be the salvation of my soul. With all my heart I praise you, O Lord my God. I will give glory to your name forever.

SCRIPTURE REFERENCES

Psalm 62:8
Psalm 22:24 NLV
Psalm 9:9 NLV
1 Peter 5:10
Psalm 63:7, 8
Psalm 73:26
1 Peter 1:6, 7
1 Peter 1:9
Psalm 86:12

TEMPTATION

God, I pray I will keep alert and pray. Otherwise temptation will overpower me. Send out your light and your truth; let them guide me. Don't let me yield to temptation, but deliver me from the evil one. You are close to all who call on you. You hear their cries for help and rescue them. Lord, you help the fallen. For you are filled with kindness. I pray I will run from anything that stimulates lust. I need to follow anything that makes me want to do right. Then I will not let sin control the way I live and not give in to its lustful desires. I confess my sins to you; I am deeply sorry for what I have done. You are faithful and just to forgive me and cleanse me from every wrong. And when I am tempted, you will show me a way out so that I will not give in to it. God, you are my only safe haven. You are a father to your children, tender and compassionate. You know the secrets of my heart. I need to be careful to make sure that my own heart is not evil and unbelieving, turning me away from you. For you my Father love me dearly. You are my loving ally and my fortress, my tower of safety, my deliverer. I give thanks to you, for you are good!

SCRIPTURE REFERENCES

Mark 14:38
Psalm 43:3
Matthew 6:13
Psalm 145:18, 19
Psalm 145:14
Psalm 145:17
2 Timothy 2:22
Romans 6:12
Psalm 38:18
1 John 1:9
1 Corinthians 10:13
Psalm 103:13
Psalm 44:21
Hebrews 3:12, 13
John 16:27
Psalm 144:2
Psalm 106:1

TITHING

God, I pray I will give you the tithes and offerings due to you. You instruct me to bring all the tithes into the storehouse, so that there will be enough food in your temple. If I do this, you will open the windows of heaven for me. You will pour out a blessing so great I won't have enough room to take it in. You tell me to try it, and you will prove it to me. Jesus teaches about money, and he says, "Don't store up treasures here on earth, store up treasures in heaven. Wherever your treasure is, there your heart and thoughts will be also." God, I pray I will not love money, for no one can serve two masters. For I will hate one and love the other, or be devoted to one and despise the other. I cannot serve both you and money. I need to not be a fool and store up earthly wealth and yet not have a rich relationship with you. You don't want me to worry about everyday life, whether I have enough food to eat and clothing. I'm not to worry whether you will provide it for me. For these things dominate the thoughts of most people, but you my heavenly father already know my needs. You will give me all I need from day to day, if I make your kingdom my primary concern. For you are great, and you do wondrous things. I thank you with all my heart.

SCRIPTURE REFERENCES

Malachi 3:8
Malachi 3:10
Matthew 6:19–21
Luke 16:13
Luke 12:21
Luke 12:29–31 NLT, NKJ
Isaiah 44:23
Psalm 111:1

TROUBLES

God, I pray I will be glad for all you are planning for me. That I would be patient in trouble, and always be prayerful. For you hear when I call to you for help. You rescue me from all my troubles. You are my hiding place, you protect me from trouble. You surround me with songs of victory. You are the source of every mercy, and you comfort me. Each day you carry me in your arms, for you have seen my troubles, and care about the anguish of my soul. I am pressed on every side by troubles, but I am not crushed or broken. I am perplexed, but I won't give up and quit. For my present troubles are quite small and won't last very long. Yet they produce for me an immeasurably great glory that will last forever! So I don't look at the troubles I can see right now, rather, I look forward to what I have not yet seen. For the troubles I see will soon be over, but the joys to come will last forever. Lord, you are my strength and fortress, my refuge in the day of trouble. With all my heart I praise you. I pray I will give glory to your name forever, for your love for me is very great.

SCRIPTURE REFERENCES

Romans 12:12
Psalm 34:17
Psalm 32:7
2 Corinthians 1:3
Psalm 68:19
Psalm 31:7
2 Corinthians 4:8
2 Corinthians 4:17, 18
Jeremiah 16:19
Psalm 86:12, 13

TRUST

God, I pray I will trust in you with all my heart, and not depend on my own understanding. That I would seek your will in all I do, and you will direct my paths. Your unfailing love surrounds those who trust in you. How precious is your unfailing love, O God. I will trust in your unfailing love forever and ever. I will trust in you at all times. I pour out my heart to you, for you are close to me when I call on you. How good it is to be near you. I will be still in your presence and wait patiently for you to act. I commit everything I do to you; I will trust you and you will help me. You alone are my refuge, my place of safety. You have never abandoned anyone who searches for you. I praise you from the bottom of my heart. Your goodness is so great! For every child of God defeats this evil world by trusting Christ to give the victory. And the ones who win this battle against the world are the ones who believe that Jesus is your Son. I pray I will cling to him and never stop trusting him.

SCRIPTURE REFERENCES

Proverbs 3:5, 6
Psalm 32:10
Psalm 36:7
Psalm 52:8
Psalm 62:8
Psalm 145:18
Psalm 73:28
Psalm 37:7
Psalm 37:5
Psalm 91:2
Psalm 9:10
Psalm 35:10
Psalm 31:19
1 John 5:4, 5
Hebrews 4:14

WISDOM

God, I pray you will give me complete understanding of what you want me to do with my life, and I ask you to make me wise with spiritual wisdom. Then the way I live will always honor and please you and I will continually do good, kind things for others. All the while, I will learn to know you better and better. You give wisdom, knowledge, and joy to those who please you. The wisdom that comes from heaven is first of all pure. It is also peace loving, gentle at all times, and willing to yield to others. It is full of mercy and good deeds. Wisdom is more precious than rubies, and nothing I desire can compare with her. She will guide me down delightful paths; all her ways are satisfying. Wisdom is a tree of life to those who embrace her; happy are those who hold her tightly. I pray I would search for wisdom as I would for lost money or hidden treasure. Then I will understand what it means to fear you, Lord, and I will gain knowledge of you. Reverence for you is the foundation of true wisdom. The rewards of wisdom come to all who obey you. You desire honesty from my heart, so you can teach me to be wise in my inmost being. I will trust in you with all my heart and not depend on my own understanding. I will carry out your instructions, for they will lead me to a fulfilled life. I will praise your name forever and ever, for you alone have all wisdom and power.

SCRIPTURE
REFERENCES

Colossians 1:9, 10
Ecclesiastes 2:26
James 3:17
Proverbs 3:15
Proverbs 3:17
Proverbs 2:4
Psalm 111:10
Psalm 51:6
Proverbs 3:5
Proverbs 4:13
Daniel 2:20

WIVES

God, I pray I will be a worthy wife, my husband's joy and crown. That I will be a virtuous and capable wife, which is worth more than precious rubies. May my husband trust me, and may I greatly enrich his life. I will not hinder him, but help him all my life. When I speak, I need my words to be wise and my conversation to be gracious. I ask you, Lord, to make me wise with spiritual wisdom, that I would live wisely and be pure. I need to be clothed with strength and dignity. I pray I will respect my husband and submit to him as I do to you Lord. May we submit to one another out of reverence for Christ. We need to give honor to each other in our marriage, and remain faithful to one another. God you will surely judge people who are immoral and those who commit adultery. You want us to be holy, so we need to keep clear of all sexual sin! Then we will control our own bodies and live in holiness and honor. A woman who fears you, Lord, will be greatly praised. I will praise you, my God and King, and bless your name forever and ever.

SCRIPTURE REFERENCES

Proverbs 12:4
Proverbs 31:10–12
Proverbs 31:26
Colossians 4:6
Colossians 1:9
Titus 2:5
Proverbs 31:25
Ephesians 5:33
Ephesians 5:22
Ephesians 5:21
Hebrews 13:4
1 Thessalonians 4:3, 4
Proverbs 31:30
Psalm 145:1

WORRIED

God, I pray I will give all my worries and cares to you, for you care about what happens to me. You tell me not to worry about anything; instead, to pray about everything. You want me to tell you what I need and thank you for all you have done. If I do this, I will experience your peace, which is more wonderful than the human mind can understand. Your peace will guard my heart and mind as I live in Christ Jesus. I pray I will not worry about having food or drink or clothing. You, my heavenly Father, already know all I need, and you will give me all I need from day to day if I live for you and make your kingdom my primary concern. So I won't worry about tomorrow. I will give you my burdens and you will take care of me. I will trust you, for my future is in your hands. You will keep me in perfect peace as I trust in you and keep my thoughts fixed on you. For I know that you cause everything to work together for my good when I love you and am called according to your purpose. I love you Lord, and I thank you for hearing and answering my prayers. How kind you are! You love me with unfailing love, and your faithfulness endures forever.

SCRIPTURE REFERENCES

1 Peter 5:7
Philippians 4:6, 7
Matthew 6:31–34
Psalm 55:22
Psalm 31:14, 15
Isaiah 26:3, 4
Romans 8:28
Psalm 116:1
Psalm 116:5
Psalm 117:2

YOUTH

God, I pray you will teach me how to live. Lead me along the path of honesty, so I will learn to be wise, and develop good judgment. That I will not turn my back on wisdom, for wisdom will protect me. I need to run from anything that stimulates my lust and follow anything that makes me want to do right. May I pursue faith and love and peace, and enjoy the companionship of those who call on you with a pure heart. I need to not let sin control the way I live and not give into its lustful desires. I pray that I will live in this evil world with self-control, right conduct, and devotion to you. You are my loving ally and my fortress, my tower of safety, my deliverer. I take refuge in you; your loved ones are precious to you. You will work out your plan for my life, for your faithful love endures forever. I will be strong and take courage, for I can do everything with the help of Christ who gives me strength. I need you to guide me along right paths, bringing honor to your name. I am blessed when I obey you and search for you with all my heart, and do not compromise with evil. I will walk only in your paths. Lord, you are wonderfully good to those who wait for you and seek you. I do seek you, Lord, and praise you, from the bottom of my heart.

SCRIPTURE REFERENCES

Psalm 27:11

Proverbs 4:5

2 Timothy 2:22

Romans 6:12

Titus 2:12

Psalm 144:2

Psalm 116:15

Psalm 138:8

Psalm 31:24

Philippians 4:13

Psalm 23:3

Psalm 119:2, 3 NLT, NIV

Lamentations 3:25

Psalm 22:26

Psalm 35:10

AUTHOR'S TESTIMONY

My first memory is when I was three years old. My mom and dad were yelling at each other in their bedroom. I was sleeping in my bed and the yelling woke me up. Shortly after that my parents got a divorce. My mother remarried soon after her divorce. Her new husband was from Turkey and he had a "dark side" that she didn't know about. My stepfather and I had a distant relationship as I grew up until I was eleven years old. Then he paid too much attention to me in a negative way. He started touching me in places he shouldn't be touching. I wanted to tell my mom, but I was afraid to because my stepfather had a temper. In the past he had hit my mom and me too. During the time he was sexually abusing me, I isolated myself from my family by staying in my bedroom with the door shut. He would come in my room anyway after my mom went to sleep. A year later I told my mom. I realized he was not going to stop and the abuse was getting worse. At first my mom asked me if I would take a lie detector test to see if I was telling her the truth. I said yes I would take the test. She eventually got my stepfather to admit that he had sexually abused me and he just laughed and said, "the jig was up." My mom and I went to the police and they wrote a report. They arrested him and put him in jail. The police found out that he was from Turkey and he was here illegally. He stayed in jail for one week and then he was released. The police said that my stepfather denied what he did to me, and in court it would be my word against his word. He moved out of our house and moved into an apartment. My mom had to carry a gun because he told her that if he couldn't have her no one could. He had no moral values. My mom remarried after her divorce. Her new husband asked my mom to send me to live with my father. My dad had a bad temper and I was scared of him. He was 6 feet, 4 inches tall and when he was mad you didn't want to say a word, or he would explode. One night he was mad at me and instead of talking to me, he grabbed my neck and threw me down the stairs. We lived in a two story house, so I was hurt by the fall, but he didn't care. I went to my room and the next day took some extra clothes to school and ran away. I didn't want to go back home and see my dad. A friend of mine told his parents where I was. They called my dad and told him I was fine. They told him they knew a family that did foster care. They asked my dad if he wanted me to go to a foster home and he said yes. My friend picked me up and took me to his parent's house. I stayed there for a few days and then moved to the foster home. The family was nice, but after a few months they called social services and requested that they find me another foster home to live in. I was sent to juvenile hall to wait until they found me another foster home. A week later I was dropped off at another home. This time the family was not very nice. I felt like they only wanted me for the money they received from the state for allowing me to live with them. One day the foster mother grabbed me by my ear and dragged me all the way home from school. I felt very humiliated and didn't want to live with the family any longer. I called a taxi cab to pick me up and take me to my grandparents' house. My grandparents called my social worker to tell her where I was and asked her to find another place for me to live. She picked me up and took me to a group placement with ten other girls. The girls were pretty wild and did things like sniffing spray paint to get high. They drank and took drugs. I had not been involved with people who drank or took drugs before. When you live in a place like this you usually do what the other girls are doing because they expect you to. I started cutting myself regularly. I liked to cut crosses on my skin. I think cutting myself was my way to deal with my inner pain. The next week I was enrolled in school. There were many gangs at the school. On the last day of school, some of the people who were in gangs would beat up a person who they didn't like for various reasons. They knew people would be too scared to tell authorities about it, or they would get beaten up too. As I was walking back to the group placement after school, I saw one of the girls I lived with surrounded by three girls. They were beating her up badly. I really didn't know what to do, but I thought to myself if some one didn't go over and help her they might kill her. Somehow I found the courage to walk across the street to help her. I knew they could beat me up badly too. But I couldn't just stand there like everyone else and act like nothing was happening. As I approached the girls, one of the girls picked up a big rock and held it up, she told me to leave, or she would hit me with it. All the girls turned their attention on me, so the girl I knew got up and starting running as fast as she could and I started running too. They chased us, but eventually they gave up. We knew we were running for our lives, so that gave us the endurance we needed to keep running as long as it took us to get away. We returned to the group placement where we lived. Because it was the last day of school we didn't have to see the girls again. At the group placement where I lived the girls liked to fight too. One girl didn't like me and she was continually trying to start fights with me. One night she was drunk and was trying to pick a fight with me. I thought to myself that tonight might be a good time to get this fight over with because she was drunk. I thought that she would pass out early in the fight. Well, I was wrong, nothing seemed to hurt her, or slow her down. The alcohol must have numbed her pain. I threw her as hard as I could against her closet door hoping she would be hurt enough to stop fighting. I was getting tired and didn't have much energy left to keep fighting and the girl didn't seem to be ready to stop fighting. I went to the night counselor's door and knocked. She opened her door and didn't say a word to me. She let me in and I slept in her room for the night. She knew that there was a fight going on, but did nothing to stop it. I was surprised that the counselor didn't try to stop the fight. I don't think she cared whether we hurt each other, got high, or anything else we did. The next day I found my hair burned in my desk drawer. It was my hair that was ripped out during the fight. Living at this place was very difficult because I never knew what would happen next. The girls had come from problems too and the way they dealt with their anger was by fighting and getting high any way they could. As time went on I starting drinking too. I liked drinking because when I drank I was happy. On the weekends we were allowed to go home to visit our families, but I had no place to go on the weekends. I got a pass to go to a girl's house that I lived with. She had an older brother and he took us to a party. I drank all night and the next day I snorted some powder up my nose. I didn't know what I was snorting, but I was too high to care. My friend and I stayed at the party all weekend long and we did not get any sleep. By the time we left the party we were exhausted. When we returned to the group placement in our bedroom were the eight girls we lived with. They were waiting for me to return. Someone had stolen one of the girl's drugs and while I was gone one of the girls said I stole them. I didn't even know anyone had any drugs. The girl who had stolen the drugs had accused me of stealing them. I said I did not steal the drugs. The girl who accused me decided to beat me up to prove I stole them and she did not. She was 5' 10" tall and weighted 160 pounds. She definitely was larger than me and she knew how to fight and I did not. I was exhausted from being gone all weekend and not getting any sleep. She pushed me on the bed and we wrestled for awhile. Then she threw me on the floor and put a pillow on my face, so I couldn't yell. She had a large wooden clog shoe and started hitting my face with the wooden shoe. She was sitting on me, so I couldn't move. She kept hitting me and I remember thinking to myself I am dying. Finally, one of the girls who was bigger than her pulled her off me. It was hard for her to get the girl off me because she had cut her wrists that day trying to commit suicide. I went to the door to leave and the girls told me to go in the bathroom and wash my face off. When I looked in the mirror I couldn't believe what I saw. My face had blood all over it and it was very swollen. It looked like I was in a terrible car accident. The girls told me to say nothing to the counselors and to leave. I left and didn't know what to do. I decided to go to my grandparents' house. I walked to the freeway and hitch hiked to their house. I had a brain concussion. I stayed there until I was well enough to go back to the group placement. My social worker came to pick me up and drive me back to the group placement. The girl that beat me up was gone. There was another girl who wanted to fight with me a few weeks later. I called my social worker and asked if I could go live with my grandparents. The next day my grandparents came to pick me up, so I could live with them. They felt sorry for me and wanted to help me. Living at the group placement was very hard emotionally and physically. I never knew what the girls would do to me next. My physical injuries had healed, but not my emotional injuries. I was in deep pain on the inside and I began to drink regularly. The alcohol temporally numbed my pain. I tried to commit suicide by drinking poison. I went to A.A. to try to stop drinking, but instead of stopping my drinking I met a guy to drink with. We went to a party in Malibu and got drunk. It was raining very hard that night. The guy drove a small Honda car and as we drove on the wet roads we spun out twice and the car turned over two times. We landed four feet from the edge of a cliff and we had no seat belts on. We were very lucky to have lived after the accident. I never saw the guy again and I kept on drinking. I started going to group counseling once a week. I would bring a cup full of alcohol to drink during the meeting. No one knew I was drinking alcohol. I would have alcohol in my locker at school and drink all day at school. No one knew I had a serious drinking problem. One night a friend and I were at Manhattan Beach pier and we were drinking a lot. The police saw us and arrested us. They took us to jail and put us in separate cells. All I could do was laugh. I was so drunk that I thought being in jail was funny, then I was sent to Juvenile Hall. My probation officer came the next day and he told me I had to go to Las Palmas Detention Camp. It was a teen prison. I had to go there because it was in my police records that I had been arrested for possession and under the influence of drugs in the past. The thought of going to Las Palmas scared me immensely and I felt hopeless. That night in my room I cried out to God to come into my life. After that I started going to the chapel services. The chaplin gave me a Bible to read and I would read the Bible every day. I was so nervous that I broke out in shingles all over my waist area. I was in a lot of pain and I had to stay in the infirmary during the day after I went to school. It was a blessing to be in the infirmary because no one could beat me up. I talked to God every night when I went to my room. I became very close to God over the next month while I waited to go to Las Palmas. I was at Las Palmas for one year and while there, I kept reading my Bible and praying. God really protected me from getting into any fights while I was living there. When it was time for me to leave my grandparents said I could live with them again. I immediately found a church with a strong teen group. I was strong for awhile and didn't get into any trouble. After about six months I met a guy who went to church with me. He lied and said he was a Christian; however, he really sold pot and drank. I fell back into my old habit of drinking. I was very disappointed in myself. I went to a counselor and he told me I was an alcoholic and that I needed to find a live-in program to stop drinking. He gave me some programs to call. I decided to go to a program that Salvation Army had. I moved to Hollywood and moved in with ten other teens that had various problems. We had group counseling every night. I was the main person that had counseling every night. I had more problems than most of the people that lived at this home. I did break some of the rules, which was a big reason they counseled me so much. But I was grateful they let me stay there and live, even though I did some wrong things. The counselors were much more caring than at any of the other places I had lived. Their kindness and understanding really helped me to change and get better. I started going back to church. I depended on God again and this time I truly recovered from my addictions. God really blessed me by having me live in a Salvation Army home. I became a happier person and much stronger emotionally and spiritually. During the time I lived at this home God taught me how to trust and depend on him. I had to change many bad habits I had learned from living in foster homes, group placements, and at Las Palmas. God used the staff at Salvation Army to help me change and become the person God wanted me to be. After one year, Salvation Army opened up a new placement home and they moved me there to help train the new counselors. I also assisted in group counseling with the teens in the home. God had made me into a new person. He saved me from alcohol, drugs, and even death. While I was living in this group placement I would look up scriptures about being brokenhearted and afraid. I was trying to find scriptures for comfort, for guidance, and for my future. Later, I found a book called, "Praying God's Will for Your Life." It has scriptures to pray for any situation that you want to pray about. I would pray scripture everyday for comfort and strength because I needed God to help me. God's word began to change my negative thoughts into his thoughts. After being in Salvation Army's program for a year and a half, I moved back home with my mother and her new husband. I started going to church and I went to a Bible study with college age people. I met a man there and we got married. My husband and I, and a friend started a Bible study in our home. The people that came were mostly in their early twenties. The Bible study kept growing larger every week. We eventually moved to a building. An assistant pastor from a church came on a Friday night to teach and decided to teach every Friday night. Later, he became the pastor of this newly formed church. The church has continued to grow and it is a large church now. The church has always reached out to people that come from all kinds of backgrounds, especially people who have had difficult lives. They have programs to help people recover from a troubled past and learn to depend on God to take care of them. I have felt very blessed to have started a church that has helped so many people. Later, I had two children that mean the world to me. They have been a real joy in my life. I have taught women's Bible studies, taken biblical counseling classes to counsel, and mentored women who are in emotional pain. I also coordinated a care giving ministry that assisted people who had an illness, or a surgery. Over the years I discovered what has encouraged people the most is praying scripture and meditating on God's word. The Bible tells us how much God loves us. We all have a desire to be loved and cared about. God is our comforter and refuge at all times. All we have to do is ask him to help us. We can face any situation life brings and God will give us the strength we need. If I didn't have God in my life I would never have been able to overcome my problems. During my life I've had struggles that have been difficult, but instead of turning back to alcohol or drugs, I have depended on God. I pray and I know that God listens to me, that he is concerned about me, and that he wants me to give him all my burdens. He doesn't want me to be troubled, or worried. He desires for me to trust him with my life and put my hope and confidence in him.

The only way I can live my life is with God; without him I am lost. He is the love of my life. Praying scripture has helped me to not get discouraged, but to have God's thoughts in my mind. He tells me not to have fear for he is with me and not to be dismayed because he is my God. That he will strengthen me and help me. God's thoughts are so much better than my thoughts. I wrote this book to help people who are hurt and need to be comforted. No matter what you've gone through God is the true answer to your problems. As you pray scripture it will bring you closer to God, his love will fill your heart and he will take care of you. As I reflect back on my painful past I see how God has used it for good. All the pain and sorrow brought me to God and to Jesus his son. God has transformed me into his precious child and he has used me to help people by encouraging them to spend time seeking to know him. He is just waiting for you to come to him.

To order additional copies of this title call:
1-877-421-READ (7323)
or please visit our Web site at
www.winepressbooks.com

If you enjoyed this quality custom-published book,
drop by our Web site for more books and information.

www.winepressgroup.com
"Your partner in custom publishing."